THE REAL
BENJAMIN
FRANKLIN

THE TRUTH BEHIND THE LEGEND

by Jessica Gunderson

COMPASS POINT BOOKS
a capstone imprint

Real Revolutionaries is published by Compass Point Books, 1710 Roe Crest Drive,
North Mankato, Minnesota 56003
www.mycapstone.com

Library of Congress Cataloging-in-Publication Data is on file with the Library of Congress.
Names: Gunderson, Jessica, author.
Title: The real Benjamin Franklin : the truth behind the legend / by Jessica Gunderson.
Description: North Mankato, Minnesota : Compass Point Books, [2019] |Series: CPB grades 4-8.
Real revolutionaries | Audience: Ages 10-14.
Identifiers: LCCN 2018042078| ISBN 9780756558932 (hardcover) |
ISBN 9780756561291 (pbk.) | ISBN 9780756558987 (ebook pdf) Subjects: LCSH: Franklin,
Benjamin, 1706-1790—Juvenile literature. | Statesmen—United States—Biography—Juvenile
literature. | Scientists—United States—Biography—Juvenile literature. | Inventors—United
States—Biography—Juvenile literature. | Printers—United States—Biography—Juvenile
literature.
Classification: LCC E302.6.F8 G86 2019 | DDC 973.3092 [B] —dc23
LC record available at https://lccn.loc.gov/2018042078

Editorial Credits
Nick Healy, editor; Sarah Bennett, designer; Eric Gohl, media researcher;
Kathy McColley, production specialist

Photo Credits
Alamy: Old Paper Studios, 32–33, Science History Images, 54, Wim Wiskerke, cover, 1;
Bridgeman Images: Look and Learn/Private Collection/Jackson, Peter, 8; Getty Images:
Bettmann, 16–17, 21, RETIRED/Apic, 23, Universal Images Group, 48–49; Granger: 24, 36,
39, 43, 45; North Wind Picture Archives: 12; Shutterstock: Atlaspix, 28; Wikimedia: Library of
Congress, 15, The White House Historical Association, 10

Design Elements
Shutterstock

Printed and bound in the USA.
PA49

Contents

CHAPTER ONE
A BUSY LIFE

*B*enjamin Franklin lived to a ripe old age, but even so, his list of accomplishments seems too long for one lifetime. He was a man of many talents, a jack-of-all-trades. Today people remember him as an author, printer, inventor, and scientist. Really, what *couldn't* the guy do? And when he wasn't busy writing and inventing, he lent his wisdom to the founding of the United States. His role among the founding fathers was so important that his picture is on our $100 bills.

Just who was Ben Franklin? He was born in Boston, Massachusetts Colony, in 1706. His father was a candle maker and a soap maker. As a teenager, Franklin went to Philadelphia to make a living as a printer. He eventually started his own printing business. On his press, Franklin printed books and pamphlets, and he became an author himself.

Franklin was interested in science and how things worked. He invented many items for daily use. His interest in electricity, as well as weather, led to his famous kite-lightning experiment. Before the Revolutionary War, he served as an agent to Great Britain, trying to maintain and repair the relationship between Great Britain and the American colonies. Eventually he became a signer of the Declaration of Independence, and he later helped craft the U.S. Constitution. His contributions to the United States earned him a prominent place as a founding father.

AN INVENTIVE MIND

In his time, Franklin's inventions helped make his name known to many in the American colonies. Often these inventions grew out of his daily needs and wishes. Swim fins, for example, were one of Franklin's first inventions. He came up with the idea of swim fins when he was about 11 years old. These devices were meant to help him swim faster. Franklin and his friends often gathered along the banks of the Charles River, where Franklin discovered his love of water. In those days, not many people knew how to swim. And people rarely swam for fun. But Franklin taught himself to swim, and he helped his friends learn how to swim too. He also often wandered the docks, watching ships sail in and out of Boston Harbor. He fancied becoming a sailor, like his older brother Josiah Jr. But when Josiah died at sea, Franklin's father tried to steer his younger son away from a life at sea. Even so, Franklin's love for swimming never faded.

When Franklin went swimming, he often thought about ways that he could swim faster. He realized that the size of people's hands and feet determined how much water they could push as they swam. If his hands and feet were bigger, he thought, he could push more water and propel himself faster in the water. He made two oval wooden paddles, or "fins," for his hands. He poked a hole in the fins for his thumbs so he could hold onto the paddles. He also strapped boards to his feet, which he called "flippers." The combination of swim fins for his hands and flippers for his feet helped him to move faster through the water.

The young Ben Franklin used wood to create devices to speed him along in the water.

His swim fins were not entirely effective, though. His wrists got sore from flapping the paddles, and the flippers were too stiff to truly mimic a fish's tail. Still, he made the best of the materials he had to work with. And his invention led to modern-day swimming fins.

SOLVING EVERYDAY PROBLEMS

Franklin was always looking for ways to make daily life easier for his fellow colonists. His inventions were geared toward everyday life. One of these inventions was the Franklin Stove. During the 1700s, fireplaces provided the source of heat for homes. But these fireplaces presented problems. Sometimes houses filled with smoke, and stray sparks from the flames could cause house fires.

In 1742, Franklin aimed to fix the problem with fireplaces and make heating more efficient. He designed what became known as the Franklin Stove. The Franklin Stove was a wood-burning stove that could be built into fireplaces. Heat and smoke from the fire would rise to warm an iron plate on top of the stove. The smoke was then carried down a channel under the wall of the hearth, and then up and out the chimney. Drawing cool air from the basement, the stove warmed it in an inner metal chamber. Then the warm air was let out into the room.

Another of Franklin's inventions solved a problem that was with him every minute of the day—his faulty vision. Franklin, like many other people, had two pairs of glasses. One was to see things far away—distance glasses. The other helped see things close up—reading glasses. He found himself often switching between the two and becoming annoyed in the process. What if, he thought, the lenses could be cut in half? The top would be for seeing far away, and the bottom would be for reading. In 1784, he had his eye doctor slice his lenses and place

Franklin created "Double Spectacles" with lower portions of the lenses for reading and top portions to clarify things in the distance.

them in one frame. He called them "Double Spectacles," but they later became known as bifocals. The invention was a success. Millions of people use bifocal lenses or other lenses based on Franklin's idea today.

Benjamin Franklin came up with many other useful inventions—an odometer that counted the rotations of carriage wheels, an extension arm to grab books off high shelves, and a library chair that could also become a step stool, to name a few. But he didn't make much money from his inventions. He didn't believe in patents. A patent is a legal right stating that only an inventor can make and sell his or her invention. Franklin believed that "As we enjoy great advantages from the inventions of others, we should be glad of an opportunity to serve others by any invention of ours." In other words, he believed that all people benefited by sharing their ideas and inventions freely.

THE WEALTH OF POOR RICHARD

An author called Richard Saunders earned Franklin the most money. Who was Richard Saunders? He was actually Benjamin Franklin.

Benjamin Franklin spent part of his youth as an apprentice in his brother's print shop, learning to run the printing press and the printing business. He was just a teenager, but he learned the business quickly and became a very skilled printer. As an adult, Franklin owned his own printing press in Philadelphia. He printed many pamphlets and newspapers, including the *Philadelphia Gazette*, which was one of the most popular newspapers in the colonies. He also printed his own work. He'd already been writing most of his life, mostly articles filled with humor and wit.

Franklin also printed and sold almanacs. An almanac is a yearly publication that contains weather forecasts, horoscopes, witty sayings, poetry, and political and scientific articles. Almanacs were popular for their daily predictions and articles. By printing them, Franklin earned a steady income. But in 1732, he found himself without an almanac to print. The author had moved on to another printer. Franklin decided to write his own.

He made up the fictional character Richard Saunders and his wife, Bridget. Under Saunders's name and using an invented personality, Franklin wrote an almanac titled *Poor Richard's Almanack*. He printed a supply of copies and offered them for sale. The volume was so popular that Franklin decided to continue. He wrote an annual almanac for 26 years. By then, the books had made him so much money that he could retire. He was only 42 years old.

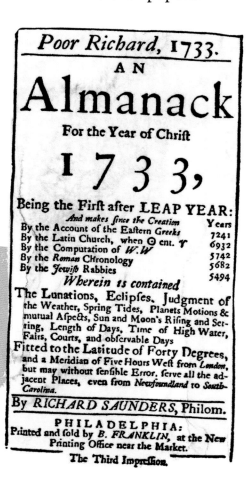

The first edition of *Poor Richard's Almanack* included bits of wisdom, such as "Snowy winter, a plentiful harvest."

In the pages of *Poor Richard's Almanack* are the witty proverbs that we associate with Benjamin Franklin. *Early to bed and early to rise makes a man healthy, wealthy, and wise. Fish and visitors smell after three days. Eat to live, and not live to eat. Three may keep a secret if two of them are dead. Well done is better than well said.*

THE BUSY CITIZEN

The success of Franklin's almanacs gave him money, and with money came the freedom to pursue other interests. Franklin started a group that met regularly to discuss philosophy. They called themselves the Junto, which means a group of people gathered for a common purpose. The Junto also discussed how to be better citizens. One of Franklin's ideas was to start a fire club.

At that time, Philadelphia had no fire department. Since most houses were made of wood, and fireplaces were used for heat and cooking, house fires were a constant danger. Franklin's idea was for the fire club to protect its members. Members vowed to help put out fires that threatened other members' homes. Each member would provide two buckets for water and several bags to save goods. The club was called the Union Fire Company. Soon, other groups started forming fire clubs around the city. In a life marked by many outstanding accomplishments, Franklin considered the fire-fighting effort his best.

Franklin and his group, the Junto, were also passionate about knowledge and learning. Franklin suggested to the group that each member bring books to share. But he wanted to provide even more books, some imported from London. Gathering those books would cost money, so Franklin recruited subscribers who would pay dues for the right to check out books. This led to the very first lending library in the colonies, called the Library Company of Philadelphia.

Later in life, Franklin also established a public hospital, called Pennsylvania Hospital, and a college, which became the University of Pennsylvania.

A REVOLUTIONARY LEADER

Last but not least are Franklin's accomplishments as a founding father. After his retirement from printing, Franklin became involved in government. He served as a councilman and a justice of the peace. In 1737, he was appointed postmaster of Philadelphia, and in 1753, he became Postmaster General of British North America. Prior to Franklin, mail was not sent out on a regular schedule. Franklin reformed the mail system, ensuring that mail was sent out at least once a week.

In 1757, he was sent to London as a representative of the Pennsylvania Assembly. He lived in London off and on for nearly 20 years. In the mid-1760s, the British government began enacting a series of laws that taxed

American colonists. Franklin spoke out against what many considered to be unfair laws, most specifically the Stamp Act of 1765. It required a tax stamp for all printed materials in the colonies. The Stamp Act stirred fury in the colonies, and, in London, Franklin testified at a meeting of the British Parliament against the Stamp Act. It was repealed one year later.

But the British taxed the colonists on other items, even though they had no representatives in British Parliament. So began the familiar cry of "No taxation without representation!" Frustrated, Franklin returned to the colonies. He helped draft the Declaration of Independence in 1776. With this document, the 13 colonies declared themselves free from the rule of Great Britain. That freedom, of course, would have to be won at war.

Benjamin Franklin and John Adams made notes on Thomas Jefferson's first draft of the Declaration of Independence. The original draft read, "We hold these truths to be sacred and undeniable." In a change often credited to Franklin, the last three words were replaced by "self-evident."

With the Revolutionary War in full swing, Franklin went to France to try to enlist that country's help. He succeeded, and the course of history was changed. In 1778, France signed a military alliance with the Americans. The French sent soldiers, supplies, and money to aid the Americans' fight against the British. France's aid helped bring about American victory.

In 1783, Franklin negotiated the peace treaty
between the British and the Americans, called the
Treaty of Paris. He then returned to Philadelphia,
where he took part in the Constitutional Convention in
1787. The Constitutional Convention was a meeting of
representatives to draft laws for the new country. Since
declaring independence, the country had been functioning

At 81 years old, Franklin
was the oldest delegate
to the Constitutional
Convention in 1787.

under laws outlined in a document called the Articles of Confederation. These governing laws had problems, though. One of the biggest issues was that the document only loosely tied the states together. The federal government had little power.

In 1787, Franklin and other delegates met in Philadelphia from May to September to replace the Articles with a new plan. The outcome was the U.S. Constitution. At the end of the convention, Franklin gave a passionate speech urging his fellow delegates to sign the document. Thirty-nine of 55 delegates signed the Constitution, and it was sent to states to be ratified, or officially accepted. On June 21, 1788, the Constitution became the official governing document of the United States.

Franklin was the only person to sign all four documents that were critical to creating the new country—the Declaration of Independence, the Treaty of Alliance with France, the Treaty of Paris, and the U.S. Constitution.

CHAPTER TWO

FRANKLIN IN LEGEND AND MYTH

A flash of lightning streaks across the sky, thunder booms, and there stands Benjamin Franklin, flying a kite in the midst of a storm. When many people today think of Benjamin Franklin, they imagine a scene like this—Franklin out flying a kite during a lightning storm with his young son next to him. And with this kite experiment, some people believe, Franklin discovered electricity.

Benjamin Franklin was an accomplished man. About that there is no doubt. But over the years, some myths have grown around this legendary figure in U.S. history. One of the greatest myths surrounding Benjamin Franklin has to do with his kite-lightning experiment. Legend has it that is how he discovered electricity.

But Franklin did not discover electricity. Not exactly. As with many stories about the founding fathers, there is some fiction mixed with fact.

FRANKLIN FLIES A KITE

This popular myth about Franklin needs to be broken down to sort out what is true and what isn't. First of all, Franklin and his son didn't just walk out into a lightning storm carrying a kite. If Franklin had done so and lightning had struck the kite, he would have been electrocuted—and probably killed. The experiment was more complicated than that.

Second, Franklin came along too late to *discover* electricity. The phenomenon of electricity was known about at the time. For years scientists had been experimenting with static electricity—electrical charges on the surface of material. (As when you rub your hair and it stands up straight. That's static electricity. The rubbing of your hair causes an electrical charge to build up.) Franklin was fascinated by electricity and conducted many small electrical experiments. He often corresponded with members of the Royal Society—a scientific organization in London.

One question on Franklin's mind was whether lightning was made up of electricity. He set out to test his theory. His first idea was to place a tall metal pole on top of a building and see if lightning was attracted to

Legends about Franklin's experiments with a kite and a key often leave out important details such as steps he took to avoid being electrocuted.

it. He described his idea in a letter to the Royal Society. But there weren't many tall buildings in the colonies, so he opted for another experiment—a kite.

One June day in 1752, Franklin saw thunderclouds rolling overhead, so he decided to try out his kite experiment. He asked his son, William, to help him. Another misconception is that William was a young boy at the time. He was actually a man in his twenties.

First, Franklin tied a silk kite to a hemp rope. The kite had a piece of wire attached to the top. The wire was meant to attract lightning. Franklin knew that the hemp rope, if wet, would carry an electrical charge. If he was holding it, he could be shocked. So he attached a silk string to the rope that he would hold onto. The silk string needed to be kept dry so he wouldn't get electrocuted.

Then he tied a metal key to the end of the hemp rope. He placed the key in a Leyden jar, which is a container used for storing electrical charges.

As the storm grew, Franklin ducked into a doorway of a barn, holding the dry silk string. The kite rose into the air. The strands of the hemp rope stood up straight, like hair charged with static electricity. Franklin was excited by this finding. He touched his knuckle to the key and felt a small electric shock. His theory had been proven. Lightning was electricity!

But little did Franklin know that just a month earlier a similar experiment had been done in Paris, France. Scientist Thomas-François Dalibard had learned about the idea Franklin sent to the Royal Society. He decided to test it out. He built a structure with a metal pole in the middle. During a thunderstorm, he observed sparks. This confirmed Franklin's theory that lightning was electricity. Dalibard wrote about the experiment, but news

Franklin suggested placing tall, pointed rods atop buildings to attract lightning that might otherwise strike the roof. A grounding wire attached to the rod would send the charge safely into the earth.

of Dalibard's successful experiment didn't reach Franklin until *after* he flew the kite.

Still, Franklin is the one credited with the discovery. And his discovery led to another invention—the lightning rod. Franklin suggested that placing a tall metal rod on top of a building would cause lightning to strike the rod, not the building. This would save buildings from getting struck by lightning and catching fire. Lightning rods became extremely popular and saved many homes and businesses from burning to the ground.

MODEL BEHAVIOR

Benjamin Franklin is often considered the model of good behavior. His *Poor Richard's Almanack* was filled with advice, such as "Clean your finger before pointing at my spots." But did Franklin actually live by his own rules? Not really. This is another myth.

One of Franklin's proverbs in the *Almanack* was "Eat to live, and not live to eat." But Franklin did not follow this advice, especially in his final years. He liked to indulge in food. And he was quite overweight late in life.

Another of Franklin's proverbs is "Early to bed and early to rise makes a man healthy, wealthy, and wise." Franklin didn't live by this rule either. He often stayed up late and slept in.

Franklin shared many bits of humor and wisdom in his almanacs, but he did not always follow his own advice.

As a young man, Franklin wanted to improve himself. He made a list of 13 virtues that he wanted to live by. Temperance, silence, order, resolution, frugality, industry, sincerity, justice, moderation, cleanliness, tranquility, chastity, and humility. Franklin had a problem following some of the virtues on his list. For example, he claimed that all things had their place, but he was messy. He left things lying around. He also forgot where he put things. In other words, he was like most people, in that he hoped and tried to be a virtuous person but he wasn't perfect.

TRULY AMERICAN

Benjamin Franklin's reputation itself is mythical. He is often called "The First American." He was a self-made man. He had his own business as a printer and that earned him a living. He was also a scientist, author, inventor, and politician. Over the centuries, he has become a folk hero.

But who was he really? In his lifetime, Franklin wore many masks. He wrote under pen names and in the voices of different characters. They included Silence Dogood; Richard Saunders; Alice Addertongue, a society gossip; and Anthony Afterwit, a man who gave humorous accounts of married life. He hid himself behind his fictional characters. Many people confuse the real Benjamin Franklin with his pen name personas.

Franklin also contributed to his own reputation with his *Autobiography.* He wrote the book late in life, and it was published after his death. In 1791, a year after his death, parts of his autobiography were published in France. In 1818, Franklin's grandson published parts of it in the United States. In 1868, the entire autobiography was published together in one volume. In it, Franklin tells tales about his youth and his various scientific and personal pursuits. But some of his stories may not be completely true. He may have exaggerated the stories to be more entertaining or to provide a lesson.

In one such tale, he wrote about a time he got into trouble as a boy. He and his friends were fishing by the Charles River in Boston. The ground was so muddy that they couldn't venture close to the water. Then Ben spotted a pile of stones nearby. He knew the stones were meant for building a house, but he proposed that the boys use them to build a wharf into the muddy riverbank.

When the builders discovered the missing stones the next day, the boys got in trouble. To try to get out of the jam, Franklin showed his father how well they had constructed their small wharf, but his father convinced him of this: "That which was not honest, could not be truly useful." The story may or may not have been rooted in truth. Franklin may have exaggerated the story to show his readers a lesson about honest work.

A TURKEY TALE

One long-standing and oft-repeated story says that Benjamin Franklin wanted the turkey, not the bald eagle, to be the national bird. This is a myth, although it has just a bit of truth to it. In 1776, after declaring independence, the founding fathers knew the new country needed an official emblem to be stamped on documents. Three men—Thomas Jefferson, John Adams, and Benjamin Franklin—were tasked with developing the Great Seal of the United States, also called the Presidential Seal.

Designing a Great Seal doesn't sound like a difficult task, but the three men struggled to agree on an emblem. They finally submitted a design that August. The design had the Eye of Providence—an ancient symbol of an eye surrounded by rays of light—and the date of independence on one side. On the other side was a shield and the Latin words *E Pluribus Unum*, meaning "Out of Many, One."

But the design was not approved by the Continental Congress. Another committee changed and added to the design. This design was not approved either. A third committee was formed. That committee asked lawyer and artist William Barton to help design the seal. Barton drew a small white eagle with wings spread.

This design was still not approved. In 1782, Charles Thomson, secretary of the Continental Congress, chose the best features of all the previous designs. He also changed the white eagle to the American bald eagle. Finally, on June 20, 1782, the Great Seal was approved by the Continental Congress. On the front is a bald eagle with wings spread, and the words *E Pluribus Unum* spelled out on ribbons from the eagle's beak. On the reverse is an unfinished pyramid and an eye above the pyramid. You might recognize this symbol—the Great Seal is printed on paper U.S. currency today.

How does the seal relate to the myth about Benjamin Franklin wanting the turkey to be the national bird? The Great Seal that Franklin, Jefferson, and Adams designed did not include a bird. When the final design was approved, making the bald eagle the national symbol, Franklin wrote a letter to his daughter. In the letter, he said, "I wish the bald eagle had not been chosen the representative of our country. He is a bird of bad moral character." He went on to say that he was "not displeased that the figure is not known as a bald eagle, but looks more like a turkey. For in truth the turkey is in comparison a much more respectable bird, and . . . a true

Franklin poked fun at the bald eagle chosen for the Great Seal of the United States.

original native of America, . . . He is besides, though a little vain and a little silly, a bird of courage, and would not hesitate to attack a grenadier of British Guards who should . . . invade his farm yard with a red coat on."

All this was said with Franklin's typical wit and humor. He didn't *really* want the turkey to be the national bird. He was, instead, poking a bit of fun at the new Great Seal and the national bird. Adding to the myth was a November 1962 cover of *The New Yorker* magazine. On the cover, artist Anatole Kovarsky drew the Great Seal with a turkey instead of an eagle, in honor of the Thanksgiving holiday. This image helped continue the Ben Franklin turkey myth.

By exploring the turkey story and other myths and half-truths, people today can better understand the real Benjamin Franklin and who he was behind the masks and myths. Clearly, he was a brilliant, complicated, and imperfect person.

CHAPTER THREE

THE UNKNOWN FRANKLIN

*B*enjamin Franklin was a man of many accomplishments and many myths. It seems we know everything about him, and then some. But there are some lesser-known truths that illuminate Franklin in ways that we may not already have seen.

Benjamin Franklin was a prominent founding father. He played an essential role in the creation of the United States. He sat alongside George Washington, Thomas Jefferson, and other founding fathers during important moments in history, such as the signing of the Declaration of Independence and the drafting of the U.S. Constitution. When you imagine those moments, you probably picture a group of old men wearing white wigs, all about the same age. But Franklin was the only one who was truly elderly. He was much older than the other founding fathers. When the Revolutionary

War broke out, he was almost 70 years old, much too old to actually fight in the war. When he signed the U.S. Constitution, he was 81 years old.

Among the founding fathers, Franklin was closest in age to George Washington, who was 26 years younger. Franklin was 49 years older than one of the youngest founding fathers, Alexander Hamilton. Maybe people should consider him a founding grandfather!

A SERIOUS SWIMMER

Long before he was a founding father, Benjamin Franklin was an avid swimmer. As a child, Franklin swam in the Charles River near Boston. He also helped his friends learn to swim. Franklin continued following his passion for swimming as an adult too. Swimming provided more than an inspiration for one of his inventions. It was a passion of his for many years, and as exercise he considered swimming "delightful and wholesome." At one time he even considered making a job of his pastime.

In 1724, at age 18, Franklin set off for London, England. Ben traveled there to buy a printing press on the advice of the governor of Pennsylvania. The plan fell through, but Franklin ended up staying in London for about a year and a half. He worked at various print shops to make a living.

In his free time, Franklin swam in the River Thames—the famous river that runs through the heart of London. At a printing house where he worked, he became friends with a young man named John Wygate. Franklin taught Wygate and another man how to swim. They both became good swimmers under Ben's instruction.

One day, Franklin was on a boat trip to Chelsea with Wygate and several others. On the way, Wygate told the group about Franklin's feats in the water. Excited by Wygate's stories, the group asked Franklin to show them. He stripped down, jumped off the boat, and set off swimming. He performed many tricks to the group's delight, both above and beneath the water. He swam alongside the boat all the way from Chelsea to Blackfriars, a distance of about 3.5 miles (5.6 kilometers). Not many people swam for fun in those days, so swimming such a distance was something unheard of.

One day a man named Sir William Wyndham came to visit Franklin. Wyndham had heard about Ben's swimming feats, and he wanted Ben to teach his sons how to swim. Wyndham also said that Franklin should start a swimming school. He could travel all over Europe and teach others how to swim.

The idea intrigued Franklin. Swimming was one of his passions, and what better way to earn a living than to teach others something he loved? But then another offer came. Franklin's friend and fellow printer, Mr. Denham, was about to set sail for Philadelphia, taking his printing press and materials with him. He wanted to start a printing business, and he wanted Franklin to work for him. Franklin had always loved the printing business too, so he decided to do it. He left behind his swimming school dreams and headed back to Philadelphia.

A 1751 depiction of the River Thames with London's Westminster Abbey in the background

But Benjamin Franklin never stopped swimming, and he never stopped teaching others. He helped others learn to swim for the rest of his life. In the 1760s, for example, Franklin offered guidance to his friend Oliver Neave, who was terrified of the water. Neave had to travel by boat a lot, which could cause anxiety for anyone who couldn't swim. Franklin wrote him a letter and gave him several tips on learning to swim.

In typical Franklin fashion, his advice about swimming was anything but dull. He told his friend to throw an egg into shallow water and watch it sink to the bottom. Then, Franklin said, try to reach into the water to retrieve it. He wrote: "In this attempt you will find, that the water buoys you up . . . that it is not so easy a thing to sink as you imagined; that you cannot, but by active force, get down to the egg." He then gave Neave useful tips on how to float. He ended by saying that Neave shouldn't rely only on floating but should "learn fairly to swim; as I wish all men were taught to do in their youth." They would, Franklin wrote, be safer, happier, and less afraid. And they would experience "the enjoyment in so delightful and wholesome an exercise."

Franklin also believed that swimming lessons should be taught at all public schools. He wrote: "Every parent would be glad to have their children skilled in swimming," and that one advantage was "to be free from the slavish terrors many of those feel who cannot swim, when they are obliged to be on the water even in crossing a ferry."

In 1968, nearly 200 years after Franklin's death, he was inducted into the International Swimming Hall of Fame.

FRANKLIN THE RUNAWAY

Another little-known fact is that Benjamin Franklin was a runaway. He ran away from home as a teenager and set out to make his own living.

Benjamin Franklin came from a huge family. His father had 17 children altogether, seven with his first wife, and 10 with his second wife. Benjamin was the youngest boy and had two sisters younger than him. For a time, the whole family was crammed into a small two-bedroom house in Boston. When Ben was 6 years old, the family moved to a larger house.

Ben's father, Josiah, wanted his youngest son to become a minister. When he was 8, Ben was sent to Boston Latin School, where his education would provide a foundation for a life as a clergyman. But after two years, the Franklin family ran out of money to pay for school, and Ben had to leave. He started learning his father's trade—making candles and soap. But Ben really disliked it. Ben's older brother James had a print shop just down the street. James printed sermons and posters, and he hoped to expand to print books. James needed a helper. So, when Ben was 12, his father sent him to work at James's print shop.

Printers in the American colonies had to be technically skilled to operate their presses, while often acting as writers and editors too.

James asked that Ben sign a nine-year apprenticeship agreement. Their father agreed. A nine-year agreement would keep Ben from running off to sea, and it would help Ben thoroughly learn the printing trade.

Ben liked the work, but his brother James was not exactly nice to him. He often beat Ben for no reason at all. He was also jealous of Ben's intelligence and wit.

To make himself less miserable, Ben read every book he could get his hands on. He also started writing. He wrote some short stories, essays, and poems that he printed and sold—which made his brother even more jealous.

James began printing and publishing a newspaper called the *New England Courant*. The *Courant* contained witty and clever essays. Ben really wanted to write one, but he knew there was no way his brother would accept it. So he disguised his handwriting, wrote an essay, and then slipped it under the printing house's door.

As it turned out, James loved the essay. It was written from the viewpoint of a female character named Silence Dogood. Her outlook on life was smart and humorous. James printed it in the *Courant*, and readers loved it. Ben wrote several more. James placed them on the front page of the newspaper. At age 16, with only two years of schooling, Ben showed his brilliance as an author.

Eventually James found out that Ben had written the Silence Dogood essays. Instead of celebrating his brother's success, James was angry and began beating Ben even more often.

James soon had larger problems. He was put in jail for printing anti-religious material in the *Courant*. He was released in less than a month, and the judge told him that he had to stop printing the *Courant* unless it was sent to a censor first. But James kept on printing. Ben continued to help his brother, but he began to fear that he would be sent to jail along with James. And he was tired of James's abuse. Ben began plotting his escape.

The easiest way to get from Boston to New York City was by boat. To raise money for a ticket aboard a boat sailing to New York, Ben sold some books. But he worried that if he bought a ticket, James might spot his name in the ship's passenger list and know where he was going. Ben sent a friend to tell a tale of woe to the ship's captain. And to give him a bribe. The friend explained that Ben was fleeing a bad romance and didn't want to be found. The captain pocketed the money and let Ben board secretly. The ship sailed away with runaway Ben aboard.

Franklin arrived in New York with only a little money to his name. He went straight to the city's only print shop and asked for a job. But the printer had a full crew of people working for him. He couldn't afford another employee. He told Ben that his son Andrew had a print shop in Philadelphia and needed a helper. So Ben decided to head to Philadelphia.

With very little money left, he bought the cheapest ticket he could find. The ship wouldn't take him all the way to Philadelphia, but he hoped to find another boat at the next stop. The ship was small and had a rotten sail. A storm came up, ripping the sail to pieces and sending the ship off course. As the ship rocked in the waves, a passenger fell overboard. Ben, an excellent swimmer who was not afraid of the water, leaned over, grabbed the man, and pulled him back in.

The captain, finding no place to land the boat, dropped anchor. The passengers had to spend the night onboard, with no food or water. The next day, the captain used a sheet as a sail, and the ship eventually landed at Perth Amboy, New Jersey.

Ben still had more than 50 miles (80 km) to go to reach Philadelphia. He set off on foot, getting soaked by a rainstorm, and then eventually found another boat. When he finally reached his destination, he was hungry and tired, and he hadn't bathed or changed clothes in days. Worse, the printer he'd come to see had already hired someone else.

But then Ben had a little good luck. Another printer in town needed help and hired him. The young runaway now had a job doing something he loved. This job would begin his career in Philadelphia as a printer and writer, which would launch his life as a leading citizen.

Franklin was alone at age 17 when he arrived in Philadelphia.

CHAPTER FOUR

CHANGING HIS MIND

*T*oday many people think of Benjamin Franklin as a person of wisdom and accomplishment. They think of him as a true American—a self-made person who rose to wealth and prominence and helped found a nation that promised liberty and equality for all people. Clearly, Franklin was a forward-thinker. He had many ideas that were ahead of his time. But his thinking wasn't always so enlightened. In some areas, his views evolved and changed over many years.

One particularly difficult truth about Franklin is that he participated in the enslavement of black people. Like Thomas Jefferson, George Washington, and other founding fathers, Franklin was a slave owner. It wasn't until very late in life that Franklin reversed his thinking on slavery. Eventually, he began to speak out in favor of abolishing slavery.

The presence of enslaved people in the American colonies traced back to before Franklin's lifetime. Slavery in the American colonies began in 1619, when a ship sailing under the Dutch flag carried enslaved people from Africa to the colony of Virginia. In the years to come, slavery would become widespread in the American colonies. Millions of African people were kidnapped and torn from their homelands. They were crowded onto ships. If they survived the voyage across the ocean, they were sold to people who forced them to work the rest of their lives without pay or any rights as human beings.

By the 1700s, slavery was common in many of the American colonies. At least 7 million Africans were brought to the colonies in the 1700s and forced to work as slaves. Slavery was most common in the South, where slaves worked on cotton, tobacco, and rice plantations. And while some Northern states banned slavery, the practice went on throughout the United States until the Civil War ended in 1865, long after Franklin's death.

Franklin, like many others at the time, accepted slavery. The work of enslaved people was valuable to the economy in the colonies. Without slaves, the colonies would not have been able to produce as much cotton, tobacco, rice, and other goods. Of course, the riches gained from these products provided no benefit to the enslaved people whose work produced them.

Franklin purchased slaves in the late 1740s and owned several slaves in his lifetime. They were made to work as his personal servants. He even brought slaves along to London in 1757, when he traveled there on behalf of the Pennsylvania assembly. Not much is known about Franklin's slaves. Franklin wrote that an enslaved man named Peter helped care for him when he was sick. He also wrote that his son's slave, King, was "often in mischief." But Franklin indicated in his will that his slaves should be freed after his death. This was very unusual at the time, since most slaveholders viewed enslaved people as valuable property that could be passed down to their children.

As a publisher, Franklin also profited from the slave trade. He sold and printed ads for slave auctions in his newspaper, the *Philadelphia Gazette*. He also profited from running ads purchased to help catch runaway slaves.

In at least one way, Franklin's attitude toward enslaved people differed from that of many white people at the time. He believed that African American children should be educated. Laws and practices at the time barred enslaved people from the simple right to learn to read and write, and even free black children were largely excluded from schools.

Even in this area, prejudice affected Franklin's thinking. At one time in his life, he thought black children were not as intelligent as white children. But an experience changed his mind. In 1763, Franklin visited a school in Philadelphia where young black children were being taught. He observed the children in school and saw

SIX POUNDS Reward.

RUN AWAY, laft night, from Bufh-town, in Baltimore county, Maryland, two convict fervant men, one named WILLIAM PITT, about 47 years of age, pitted with the fmall-pox, about fix feet high; had on, and took with him, a brown half worn furtout coat; two white fhirts, an ozenbrigs frock, with buttons on the fhoulder, a pair of trowfers, yarn ftockings, fmall old felt hat, half boots, with iron plates round the heels, and a pair of old fhoes, with nails in the heels, a pair of greafy leather breeches; he wears his own fhort grey curled hair, and fpeaks on the Weft country dialect; he fays he is a Tallow-chandler and Horfe-jockey. The other named EDWARD WILLIAMS, a Cooper by trade, about 40 years of age, is a down-looking ftout fellow, of a dark complexion, the fore part of his head fhaved, and the back part fhort brown hair, and fpeaks much on the Weft country dialect; had on a new felt hat, a white fhirt, a white fuftian frock, lined with white flannel, a brown cloth jacket, dirty coarfe trowfers, yarn ftockings, and half worn fhoes. Whoever takes up the above fervants, and fecures them in any goal, or brings them to the fubfcribers, fhall receive, if 10 miles and under 40 miles from home, FORTY SHILLINGS, befides what the law allows, and if a greater diftance, the above reward, paid by

WILLIAM YOUNG, junior, RICHARD RUFF.

N. B. They have not been above four weeks in the country. July 12, 1773.

To be SOLD by
JOHN JARMAN,
At his STORE in Third-ftreet, between Arch and Race-ftreets, oppofite Cherry-Alley,

MUSCOVADO SUGARS, in hogfheads, barrels or leffer quantity, loaf and lump ditto, Jamaica fpirits, Weft-India and New-England rum, by wholefale and retail, melaffes by ditto, French and Carolina indigo, beft green, fuchong and bohea tea, chocolate and coffee, ginger in kegs, allom, copperas, brimftone, ground redwood, madder, brazilletto and logwood, nutmegs, mace, cinnamon and cloves, powder, fhot and lead, pepper, alfpice, Wefton's fnuff in bottles, foap by the box, and cotton by the bale or lefs quantity; alfo Rhode-Ifland cheefe, &c. &c.------ All which he will fell on the loweft terms.------Orders from the country will be punctually obferved and complied with.   Tbc.

To be RENTED, for a Term of Years,

THE MILLS at the Falls of James River, in the Town of Manchefter, which confift of a double Saw-mill and Grift-mill, with two Pair of Stones, for Country Work, which is worth about 400 Barrels of Corn the Year, a Merchant-mill with four Pair of beft French Burr Stones, and all Conveniencies neceffary for carrying on the manufacturing Bufinefs in the beft

Franklin's newspaper included paid advertisements offering rewards for capturing enslaved people who had fled to freedom. If captured, escaped slaves often faced violent punishment.

how smart they were. He realized that he'd been wrong. Black children were just as intelligent as white children, Franklin concluded. He wrote that "Their apprehension seems as quick, their memory as strong, and their docility in every respect equal to that of white children."

But even with this truth clear in his mind, he continued owning slaves. As time went on, he began questioning whether slavery was right. He felt the British were, in some ways, enslaving the American colonists by not allowing them representation in government. That was wrong, he thought, and slavery as a whole was wrong.

After the Revolutionary War, when Franklin was helping draft the U.S. Constitution, the subject of slavery caused division and disagreement. Delegates to the Constitutional Convention debated whether slavery should be allowed in the new country. Many delegates from the South said they would refuse to join the United States if slavery wasn't going to be legal. Antislavery delegates proposed a ban on the slave trade. The issue caused so much arguing that the men eventually compromised. The slave trade could remain legal for another 20 years. During all of this debate, Benjamin Franklin didn't take much of a stand either way.

But by the end of his life, Franklin became a true abolitionist. In 1787, he became the president of an antislavery group called the Pennsylvania Society for Promoting the Abolition of Slavery. In 1780, the Society had influenced Pennsylvania to become the first state to pass laws for the gradual elimination of slavery. When he became president of the society, Franklin believed that gradually ending slavery was the best course. He thought ending slavery all at once might cause problems for newly freed slaves. But then he began to change his mind, believing that slavery should be completely abolished.

In 1789, he wrote and published several essays against slavery. He called slavery "an atrocious debasement of human nature." In 1790, he petitioned Congress to end slavery. Congress dismissed the petition, but one thing was clear: Benjamin Franklin had made a turnaround from a slaveholder to an abolitionist who believed in liberty and equality for enslaved people.

AN ADDRESS

To the PUBLIC,

FROM THE

Pennsylvania Society for promoting the Abolition of Slavery, and the Relief of Free Negroes, unlawfully held in Bondage.

I T is with peculiar satisfaction we assure the friends of humanity, that in prosecuting the design of our association, our endeavours have proved successful, far beyond our most sanguine expectations.

Encouraged by this success, and by the daily progress of that luminous and benign spirit of liberty, which is diffusing itself throughout the world; and humbly hoping for the continuance of the divine blessing on our labors, we have ventured to make an important addition to our original plan, and do therefore, earnestly solicit the support and assistance, of all who can feel the tender emotions of sympathy and compassion, or relish the exalted pleasure of beneficence.

Slavery is such an atrocious debasement of human nature, that its very extirpation, if not performed with solicitous care, may sometimes open a source of serious evils.

The unhappy man who has long been treated as a brute animal, too frequently sinks beneath the common standard of the human species. The galling chains that bind his body, do also fetter his intellectual faculties, and impair the social affections of his heart. Accustomed to move like a mere machine, by the will of a master, reflection is suspended; he has not the power of choice; and reason and conscience, have but little influence over his conduct: because he is chiefly governed by the passion of fear. He is poor and friendless——perhaps worn out by extreme labor, age and disease.

Under such circumstances, freedom may often prove a misfortune to himself, and prejudicial to society.

Attention to emancipated black people, it is therefore to be hoped, will become a branch of our national police; but as far as we contribute to promote this emancipation, so far that attention is evidently a serious duty, incumbent on us, and which we mean to discharge to the best of our judgment and abilities.

To instruct; to advise; to qualify those who have been restored to freedom, for the exercise and enjoyment of civil liberty. To promote in them habits of industry; to furnish them with employments suited to their age, sex, talents, and other circumstances; and to procure their children an education calculated for their future situation in life. These are the great outlines of the annexed plan, which we have adopted, and which we conceive will essentially promote the public good, and the happiness of these our hitherto too much neglected fellow creatures.

A Plan so extensive cannot be carried into execution, without considerable pecuniary resources, beyond the present ordinary funds of the society. We hope much from the generosity of enlightened and benevolent freemen, and will gratefully receive any donations or subscriptions for this purpose, which may be made to our treasurer, James Starr, or to James Pemberton, chairman, of our committee of correspondence.

Signed by order of the Society,

B. FRANKLIN, President.

Philadelphia, 9th of November, 1789.

Franklin's views on slavery changed with time. In 1789, he signed an address calling for it to be abolished.

A LOYAL SUBJECT

Nicknamed "The First American," Benjamin Franklin ranks among the people who came to personify the American spirit. That spirit represented liberty, equality, and self-government. It rejected the crown and the power of a distant empire. But an unexpected truth is that Benjamin Franklin was perhaps not as purely American as people today assume.

In fact, he was a reluctant revolutionary. He lived in London and loved it, and for quite some time he wanted to remain loyal to the English crown.

In 1757, Franklin was sent to London as a representative of the Pennsylvania Assembly. His goal was to settle a tax dispute between the colonists and the British owners of the Pennsylvania Colony. Franklin was excited to go "home" to England, as he put it. London was a large city, much larger than Philadelphia. Philadelphia had fewer than 25,000 residents, and London had 750,000. Franklin found himself enthralled with the many shops, social clubs, and theaters of London. He had planned to stay for a brief time, but he ended up living in London for five years before returning to Pennsylvania.

While there, he became famous. Franklin's portraits sold by the dozens. He also loved royalty, and he attended King George III's coronation in 1761. He considered himself a true Englishman. In one of his writings, he said that he had "respect for the mother country, and admiration of everything that is British."

In 1762, Franklin returned to Philadelphia for two years to settle some of his business affairs. But he longed to return to London and settle there forever. In 1764, he made his return to London. By that time, American colonists were becoming upset with the taxes that the British were making them pay.

Franklin was in London when Great Britain enacted the Stamp Act of 1765, which enraged many colonists. The Stamp Act required that all printed documents in the colonies must have an expensive stamp on them. The money would go directly to England. A group called the Sons of Liberty formed in Boston and New York with the purpose of protesting the Stamp Act. They threatened to burn down the office of a stamp distributor. They also attacked the homes of other government officials.

Franklin thought the colonists were overreacting. But he wanted to calm the tensions between the American colonists and the British authorities. He advised the British Parliament to drop the Stamp Act. In 1766, the British government did get rid of the Stamp Act, but a rift between the colonies and Great Britain remained.

In the American colonies, colonists began thinking about separating from Great Britain, or at least rebelling until England stopped imposing taxes and laws on them. Franklin still believed that the American colonies should remain part of the British empire. He pushed for colonial representation in the British government, thinking that might solve the problem.

At the same time, Franklin was hoping to gain a position in the British government and make London his home for good. In 1768, British leaders created a government department dedicated to American affairs, and they were considering giving Franklin a leading position in the department. Franklin was excited by this prospect. He said it was "agreeable to me to remain among [British friends] some time longer, if not for the rest of my life." But, to Franklin's disappointment, the British authorities passed him over for someone else.

Before the Revolutionary War, Franklin lived in London for long stretches and tried to settle disputes between the American colonies and their distant rulers.

During this time, more British laws upset people in the American colonies. In 1767, the British passed the Townshend Acts, a series of laws that taxed the American colonists. Then, in 1773, the British passed the Tea Act, which taxed the Americans on all tea imported from England. Many colonists felt outraged, and the Sons of Liberty protested the Tea Act in the famous Boston Tea Party in December 1773. A group of men disguised themselves as Mohawk Indians, raided three ships, and dumped hundreds of chests of tea into the river.

In London, Franklin struggled to mend the rift between the colonies and Great Britain. In 1772, he received a packet of letters from an unnamed sender. The packet held letters written by Thomas Hutchinson, colonial governor of Massachusetts. Hutchinson wrote to English authorities, describing the colonists' rage over what they saw as unfair laws. He requested more British troops in the colonies to control the angry citizens.

Franklin decided to send the letters to Samuel Adams, the head of the Massachusetts Committee of Correspondence. Telling Adams not to publish the letters, Franklin said he should share them with other leaders in the colonies. Franklin thought the colonists would blame the colonial leaders like Hutchinson, rather than the British government, for the problems between the colonies and the British. This way, Franklin hoped, the situation might be calmed.

Franklin's plan backfired. The letters were published, and many colonists became even more angry at the British. They felt there was a conspiracy against their rights. And then the British government turned against Franklin. They blamed him for exposing the letters and increasing the tension between the colonies and England.

Franklin was humiliated, but he still tried to mend the American-British relationship. He offered to pay out of his own pocket the cost of tea thrown into Boston Harbor. He tried to get the British to stop the Coercive Act of 1774, which closed Boston's harbor as a punishment for the Tea Party. But the British wouldn't listen to him. One official even called him "one of the bitterest enemies […] this country has ever known."

This was the last straw for Franklin. He sailed for America on March 20, 1775, and he became an American patriot. He fully supported American independence and signed the Declaration of Independence.

So, Benjamin Franklin was a true American now, right? Not exactly. In 1776, Franklin went to France to serve as ambassador. He lived there for eight years, and he came to love it. He wanted to stay. He proposed marriage to a Frenchwoman named Anne-Catherine Helvetius, but she turned him down. Still, in 1784, he wrote: "I am here among a people that love and respect me […] perhaps I may conclude to die among them." He added that he felt he'd become "a stranger in my own country."

But when Franklin's ambassadorship concluded in 1785, he returned, somewhat reluctantly, to Philadelphia. He had spent most of his adult life living abroad. Although he seemed to prefer Europe to America, he remained a leading citizen in the United States. He helped craft the Constitution, which became the foundation of a durable government by and for the people.

CHAPTER FIVE
FRANKLIN'S LASTING LEGACY

As an author, businessman, and statesman, Benjamin Franklin made himself famous and made his community and his country a better place. His work affected the daily lives of individuals as well as the relationships between countries of the world. But perhaps his greatest genius and most ground-breaking work came in the sciences. His studies and experiments helped explain how the world works—in ways visible and invisible.

Franklin's interest in electricity began a few years before his kite-lightning experiment. In 1743, Franklin was visiting Boston, where he attended an electric magic show. At the time, no one knew much about electricity. Traveling "electricians" would wow crowds with magic tricks. One trick involved suspending a boy from the ceiling with silk threads. Then the electrician would rub the boy's feet with a glass tube. Sparks would fly, and crowds would cheer. When these tricks were performed, no one really understood what caused the sparks, not even the so-called electricians. Franklin decided he wanted to find out why this happened.

It turns out the sparks were caused by static electricity. After seeing the electric show, Franklin did some experiments of his own with static electricity. In Franklin's day, scientists believed electricity involved two fluids (called vitreous and resinous), but Franklin concluded that electricity involved actually just one fluid with two different pressures. He labeled the two pressures "positive" and "negative." He also discovered that certain materials carried electrical charges more than others. He called these "conductors." These terms are still used today in the field of electricity.

Franklin broke new ground in other ways. He developed what is called the Law of Conservation of Electric Charge. He observed that electricity could not be created. Instead, it could only be *collected*. In one experiment he lined up several plates of glass sandwiched between lead plates and connected with wires. He called it an electric battery. In fact, he had created the very first electrical battery.

For his electrical theories and experiments, Franklin received the British Copley Medal in 1753. He was the first person living outside Great Britain to receive the medal. His contributions to the field are recognized in another way: A measurement of electricity is named after him—the franklin.

Franklin's achievements as a scientist were every bit as important as his work as a statesman, and his discoveries and inventions changed the lives of Americans for generations to come.

Franklin also had an interest in health and the human body. During his lifetime, many ideas about illness and disease were based on superstition. One belief was that people caught colds from being cold or wearing wet clothes. But Franklin didn't think people caught colds from being cold. He observed during his winter travels that he would get very cold, but he didn't catch a cold. He also knew that swimming didn't make someone catch a cold either. So if moisture and cold weather didn't make someone catch a cold, then what did?

Franklin came up with a theory that no one had thought of before. He noted how colds move between people. He wrote, "People often catch cold from one another when shut up together in small close rooms, coaches, and when sitting near [each other]." He was right. We now know that cold viruses spread between people.

His talent for forward-thinking also showed in his belief that exercise helped people stay healthy. He thought that fresh air and outdoor exercise kept people from getting sick. Franklin observed that one benefit of exercise was to help blood circulation. In a letter to his son, he described a plan for vigorous exercise. He said it was better to walk for 1 mile (1.6 km) than to ride a horse for 5 miles (8 km). He also advised lifting weights. His ideas about exercise were very new. At that time, people didn't exercise regularly as they do today.

Franklin's interest in science also showed in his curiosity about the weather. In October 1743, he set out to observe the lunar eclipse in Philadelphia. But then a storm blew in, and he was unable to see the eclipse. He noticed that the winds from the storm were blowing from the northeast. Later he heard that people in Boston—northeast of Philadelphia—were able to see the eclipse. The storm didn't arrive there until much later. He wondered how this could be. Since the winds blew from the northeast, he assumed the storm came from the northeast. But in fact, it came from the opposite direction.

Curious, Franklin began tracking the movement of storms. He discovered that storms can move in the opposite direction of the wind. He began digging deeper into why that might be. He theorized that the movement of storms has to do with high pressure and low pressure, not the direction of the wind. His theory was a huge advancement in the field of meteorology—the study of weather and weather patterns. His ideas allowed for meteorologists to predict the weather and when a storm would arrive.

Another weather phenomenon that puzzled Franklin was hailstorms in the summer. How could pieces of ice fall from the sky when it was hot outside? He developed a theory. He thought that the air in the upper atmosphere was colder than the air in the lower atmosphere. So, he believed, when moisture developed in the upper atmosphere, it froze. The frozen pellets—hail—fell so fast through the lower atmosphere that they didn't have time to melt. He had no way to test his theory, but it turns out he was correct.

Franklin's scientific contributions didn't stop there. He also discovered the Gulf Stream. In his travels, he went on eight voyages across the Atlantic Ocean. On his first trip in 1724, he tested the water temperature. He noticed that the water was much warmer in some areas than others. He continued testing the water at various depths and places on the rest of his voyages. He realized that there was a warm current that ran like a river over the ocean. The current ran from west to east. He named it the Gulf Stream, and he drew a mostly accurate map of its path.

Why was this important? He advised that ship captains should follow the Gulf Stream if they were sailing west to east. But if traveling east to west, ships should avoid it, he said, because the current slowed them down. At first, no one followed his advice. But many years later, ship captains began routing their ships based on the Gulf Stream. Avoiding the Gulf Stream when traveling westward shaved two weeks off the ships' sailing time.

Benjamin Franklin was many things—a printer, an author, a founding father, and a diplomat. He helped to make the United States into an independent, democratic country. But his scientific achievements set him apart from his fellow founding fathers. He had ground-breaking theories about electricity, weather, ocean currents, and health and the human body. These theories enlightened other scientists who came after him. Franklin's curiosity helped shape the world we live in today.

TIMELINE

JANUARY 17, 1706
Benjamin Franklin is born in Boston, Massachusetts.

1718
Franklin becomes an apprentice at his brother James's print shop.

1724
Franklin travels to London, England, to buy supplies to start his own printing press shop. He stays in London for two years.

1728
Franklin opens his own printing press business in Philadelphia, Pennsylvania.

1732
Franklin publishes the first volume of *Poor Richard's Almanack*.

1742
Franklin invents the Franklin Stove, a heating device that could be inserted into a fireplace.

1752
Franklin and his son William conduct the famous kite-lightning experiment.

1757
Franklin goes to London as an agent for the Pennsylvania Colony.

1765
Great Britain passes the Stamp Act, requiring colonists to place a paid stamp on all printed documents. Franklin testifies in London against the Stamp Act.

DECEMBER 16, 1773
The Sons of Liberty protest the Tea Act of 1773 by throwing tea into the Boston Harbor.

MARCH 1775
Franklin leaves London and sails back to the colonies.

APRIL 1775

American militia clash with British troops in the
Battles of Lexington and Concord. These battles are
the beginning of the Revolutionary War.

JULY 4, 1776

Franklin signs the Declaration of Independence.
The document officially declares that the colonies
are independent from Great Britain.

DECEMBER 1776

Franklin goes to France as ambassador.

1778

Franklin negotiates the Treaty of Alliance with France. France
aligns with the United States and declares war on Great Britain.

OCTOBER 19, 1781

British General Charles Cornwallis surrenders
to American General George Washington.

1783

Franklin signs the Treaty of Paris, officially ending
the Revolutionary War.

1785

Franklin returns to the United States.

1787

Franklin helps draft the U.S. Constitution.

1790

Franklin presents a petition to the U.S. Congress to end slavery.
Congress dismisses the petition.

APRIL 17, 1790

Benjamin Franklin dies at age 84 in Philadelphia. His body is
buried in Christ Church Burial Ground in Philadelphia.

GLOSSARY

abolitionist—a person who supported the banning of slavery

ambassador—a government official who represents his or her country in a foreign country

apprentice—a person who works for and learns from a skilled professional for a set amount of time; this time period is known as the apprenticeship

atmosphere—the layer of gases that surrounds Earth

emblem—a device, symbol, design, or figure used as an identifying mark

negotiate—to handle a matter through discussion and compromise, rather than by force

patent—the right to be the only one to make, use, or sell an invention for a certain number of years

persona—a character assumed by an author in written works

phenomenon—a fact, feature, or event of scientific interest

philosophy—the study of logic, ethics, and natural laws to achieve wisdom

proverb—a short saying that expresses a truth or offers advice

virtue—a desirable quality

FURTHER READING

Fleming, Thomas J. *Ben Franklin: Inventing America*. Minneapolis, MN: Voyageur Press, 2016.

Morlock, Theresa. *20 Fun Facts about Benjamin Franklin*. Fun Fact File: The Founding Fathers New York: Gareth Stevens Publishing, 2017.

Quirk, Anne. *The Good Fight: The Feuds of the Founding Fathers (and How they Shaped the Nation)*. New York: Alfred A. Knopf, 2017.

INTERNET SITES

Use FactHound to find Internet sites related to this book.

Visit *www.facthound.com*

Just type in 9780756558932 and go.

SOURCE NOTES

p. 11, "As we enjoy…" Benjamin Franklin. *The First Scientific American: Benjamin Franklin and the Pursuit of Genius.* New York, NY: Basic Books, 2006.

p. 26, "That which was not honest…" Benjamin Franklin. *The Autobiography of Benjamin Franklin.* London, England: George Bell & Sons, 1884. p. 8.

p. 28, "I wish the bald eagle…" Benjamin Franklin. "American Myths: Benjamin Franklin's Turkey and the Presidential Seal" by Jimmy Stamp. *Smithsonian Magazine,* January 25, 2013.

p. 34, "In this attempt…" Benjamin Franklin. "Useful Hints for Learning to Swim. By Benjamin Franklin, LL. D. F. R. S. In a Letter to a Friend." *Town & Country Magazine,* Or, Universal Repository Of Knowledge, Instruction & Entertainment 12, (February 1780): 76-78. American Antiquarian Society (AAS) Historical Periodicals Collection: Series 1, EBSCOhost. p. 77–78.

p. 34, "Every parent would be…" Benjamin Franklin. International Swimming Hall of Fame Honorees. https://ishof.org/benjamin-franklin-(usa).html Accessed September 18, 2018.

p. 42, "often in mischief." Benjamin Franklin. *Benjamin Franklin.* New Haven, CT: Yale University Press, 2002. p. 105.

p. 44, "Their apprehension…" Benjamin Franklin. *The Americanization of Benjamin Franklin.* New York, NY: Penguin Press, 2004. p. 226.

p. 45, "an atrocious…" Benjamin Franklin. *The Americanization of Benjamin Franklin.* New York, NY: Penguin Press, 2004. p, 227.

p. 51, "one of the bitterest enemies…" and "I am here among…" Benjamin Franklin. *The Americanization of Benjamin Franklin.* New York, NY: Penguin Press, 2004. p. 150 & 209.

p. 55, "People often catch…" Benjamin Franklin. *The First American: The Life and Times of Benjamin Franklin.* New York, NY: Doubleday, 2000. p. 446.

SELECT BIBLIOGRAPHY

Brands, H.W. *The First American: The Life and Times of Benjamin Franklin*. New York, NY: Doubleday, 2000.

Chaplin, Joyce E. *The First Scientific American: Benjamin Franklin and the Pursuit of Genius*. New York, NY: Basic Books, 2006.

Franklin, Benjamin. *The Autobiography of Benjamin Franklin*. London, England: George Bell & Sons, 1884.

Franklin, Benjamin. "Useful Hints for learning to Swim. By Benjamin Franklin, LL. D. F. R. S. In a Letter to a Friend." *Town & Country Magazine*, Or, Universal Repository Of Knowledge, Instruction & Entertainment 12, (February 1780): 76-78. American Antiquarian Society (AAS) Historical Periodicals Collection: Series 1, EBSCOhost.

International Swimming Hall of Fame. https://ishof.org/benjamin-franklin-(usa).html

Isaacson, Walter. *Benjamin Franklin: An American Life*. New York, NY: Simon & Schuster, 2003.

Morgan, Edmund S. *Benjamin Franklin*. New Haven, CT: Yale University Press, 2002.

PBS. Benjamin Franklin. http://www.pbs.org/benfranklin/index.html

Stamp, Jimmy. "American Myths: Benjamin Franklin's Turkey and the Presidential Seal." https://www.smithsonianmag.com/arts-culture/american-myths-benjamin-franklins-turkey-and-the-presidential-seal-6623414/

Weinberger, Jerry. *Benjamin Franklin Unmasked: On the Unity of His Moral, Religious, and Political Thought*. Lawrence, KS: University Press of Kansas, 2005.

Wood, Gordon S. *The Americanization of Benjamin Franklin*. New York, NY: Penguin Press, 2004.

INDEX